The Chosen Ones

Angelic-Human Hybrids

Michael Love

Sacred Light Publishing

First Printing, 2025

Contents

Dedication

To Lara—my guiding light in every shadowed valley and every mountain climbed. Your fierce love, unshakable faith, and quiet strength have been the unseen hands that lifted me when I faltered. This creation exists because your spirit walked beside mine through every word, every doubt, and every breakthrough. This book is not just mine—it is ours, etched with love, fire, and destiny.

To the luminous Starseeds scattered across this planet as well: your presence, your resonance, your courage to awaken have fueled this mission. You are the hidden choir behind these pages, singing a truth the world is just beginning to hear.

In deep love and cosmic gratitude,
Michael Love

Forward

There are very special beings walking the Earth today—beings who appear human, yet carry within them the light of worlds. You may be one of them. You've always sensed something different. This book will confirm what your soul has always known.

This is not just a book. It is a transmission.

It calls out to the Chosen Ones—those who came here with a divine mission encoded into their very DNA. The ones who have always stood at the edge of reality, feeling the pulse of something greater. The ones who walk between worlds, who see the signs, who feel the frequencies.

You didn't imagine it. You didn't make it up.
You came from the stars.
You answered the call.
And now… it's time to remember.

Every chapter in this book is a key to awakening—unlocking pieces of your memory, your purpose, your power. From your celestial origins to your sacred mission, from the divine trials to the supernatural strength you've

Chapter 3 The Sacred Archetypes – Emissaries of Light

Healers and Restorers

Among the most vital emissaries sent to Earth were the Healers—Angelic-Human hybrids encoded with powerful frequencies of restoration. These beings did not come with scalpels or prescriptions. They came carrying the raw, unfiltered essence of divine energy—the living light of remembrance. Their presence alone brings calm where there was chaos, peace where there was pain, clarity where there was confusion.

Healers were not assigned arbitrarily. They were chosen from soul lineages with ancient ties to the crystalline healing temples of Lyra, Sirius, and Andromeda. In the higher realms, they mastered the language of light and sound, learned how to move energy through intention, and carry divine resonance in their very touch, voice, and gaze.

Their healing is often subtle, yet undeniably powerful. They awaken dormant energy in others, clearing lifetimes of trauma with a single conversation, or soothing emotional wounds simply by being near. Some healers emit frequencies that calm entire rooms. Others activate deep emotional releases, triggering spontaneous spiritual breakthroughs in those around them. Their energy fields operate like tuning forks, bringing diseased or distorted frequencies back into harmony.

Some work with their hands, others through sound, intuition, or simply presence. But all of them carry a frequency that reminds the soul what wholeness feels like. They do not just treat symptoms—they reconnect others to their divine blueprint. They restore what the world has broken, realigning the body, mind, and spirit with the higher self.

You will know a true healer not by what they say—but by what you feel in their presence. And if this resonance lives within you… then you, too, may be one of these sacred restorers, walking silently but powerfully among the wounded, carrying a light that cannot be extinguished.

Teachers and Prophets

Among the ranks of the Chosen Ones are the Teachers and Prophets—those encoded with divine memory and spiritual insight, sent to Earth to awaken the sleeping and remind humanity of its forgotten truth. These beings are not ordinary educators. They are transmitters of cosmic knowledge, vessels through which the wisdom of higher realms flows into the density of this world.

The Teachers carry within them sacred understandings—truths that stretch far beyond books or human philosophies. Their knowledge was not learned—it was remembered. They teach not to impress, but to activate. Their words ignite the dormant codes within others, awakening curiosity, clarity, and deep spiritual yearning. Some speak boldly to the many. Others whisper quietly to the few. But their messages always stir something ancient within the soul.

The Prophets are visionaries—those who see beyond time. They are shown glimpses of what is to come, not as predictions of fate, but as timelines waiting to be chosen. Their dreams, visions, and downloads come directly from Source or through the celestial councils they are connected to. They speak of the fall of false systems, the rising of the New Earth, the reunification of soul families, and the awakening of the divine human.

Many times, their words are met with doubt or dismissal—but still they speak, because the message is greater than the messenger.

Common themes shared by these Teachers and Prophets include:

"You are not just human."

"You are powerful beyond belief."

"The illusion is crumbling."

"Your awakening is the beginning of the world's transformation."

They guide others back to their own divine sovereignty, urging humanity to remember what it truly is—not victims of fate, but creators of reality. Their mission is not to be worshipped, but to remind others of the light they carry within.

And if you've ever felt the burning truth inside you, the kind that won't let you stay silent… then you may be one of them. One who came not just to witness the shift, but to speak it into being.

Warriors and Guardians

Not all who came to Earth did so to teach or heal. Some came to stand between the light and the darkness—to defend, to shield, and to protect. These are the Warriors and Guardians, Angelic-Human hybrids forged in the fires of cosmic battle, encoded with divine authority to confront the forces that seek to enslave consciousness and suppress truth.

The Warriors are not violent—but their presence is commanding. Their energy disrupts darkness wherever it hides. They don't need to lift a weapon—their very frequency is a weapon. They carry codes of divine justice and uncompromising truth, and when awakened, they become immovable forces that shatter illusion and dissolve fear. They walk boldly, speak powerfully, and often find themselves targeted by the very systems they came to dismantle. And still—they do not back down.

The Guardians are protectors—sentinels of light who hold energetic boundaries around people, places, and sacred missions. Many serve in silence, watching over timelines and shielding souls from unseen attacks. Others guard sacred knowledge, ancient codes, or powerful spiritual sites. Some are assigned to individuals—ensuring their activation unfolds at the right time, in the right way. Wherever they are, darkness cannot thrive.

Together, Warriors and Guardians are spiritual stabilizers—ensuring the planet's ascension timeline remains intact. They challenge falsehood. They expose corruption. They protect those who carry light until they are strong enough to shine on their own.

Their battles are often invisible—but the results are not. Entire systems shift when these beings take their place. Spiritual attacks dissolve. Energetic blocks are broken. The truth finds a voice.

If you've always felt a deep urge to protect, to defend truth, or to push back against injustice—even at great personal cost—you may be one of them. Not here for peace, but to make way for it. Not here to avoid the darkness, but to walk straight into it—and light it up from the inside.

Messengers and Shepherds

Among the Chosen Ones walk the unseen guides—the Messengers and Shepherds—those who move between the higher and lower realms, carrying transmissions of light to awaken the human soul. Their mission is not always to speak loudly, but to speak clearly. Not to lead with force, but to lead with presence. These are the ones who guide humanity gently through signs, symbols, and divine timing.

Messengers serve as living bridges between dimensions, tuned to frequencies beyond ordinary perception. They receive downloads from higher realms and relay them in subtle yet powerful ways—through conversations, creative expression, dreams, or spontaneous insight.

They don't always know how or why the messages arrive, but they feel when they must be shared. Often, they speak exactly what someone needs to hear at exactly the right moment. They are the carriers of synchronicity.

Their signs may appear as repeating numbers like 11:11, 222, or 144, animal totems, sudden coincidences, or words spoken by strangers that strike the soul. These aren't accidents—they are activations, orchestrated by Messengers working behind the scenes to awaken others to their path.

Shepherds are the heart-guides—those who walk with others, not in front of them. They don't push; they gently call others forward with wisdom, patience, and love. Shepherds are here to guide souls through the transition from asleep to awakened, from lost to aligned. They see potential where others see problems, and they remain steady even when those they lead falter. Their presence alone becomes a safe harbor during spiritual storms.

Both Messengers and Shepherds help people remember who they are. They don't demand awakening—they inspire it. They are the compass and the comforter, showing the way when the path becomes unclear.

If you've ever felt that mysterious pull to be in the right place at the right time, to speak words you didn't plan but felt destined to say, or to walk beside others during their awakening—you may be one of them.

You are not just a voice.

You are a signal.

A lighthouse.

A signpost from the stars.

Sages, Creators, and Mystics

There are some Chosen Ones whose very essence radiates ancient memory, vision, and transcendence. These are the Sages, Creators, and Mystics—each uniquely encoded to play a pivotal role in the elevation of human consciousness. While their missions differ, all three archetypes serve as conduits between what is and what can be. They are not here to blend into the world—they are here to reshape it from the inside out.

Sages are the wisdom bearers. They carry the ancient memory of civilizations long lost and truths buried beneath layers of time. The Sage's knowledge is not learned—it is remembered. Their words carry weight not because of their authority, but because of the timeless resonance behind them. Sages speak of sacred geometry, cosmic law, divine cycles, and forgotten origins. They are keepers of mysteries, guardians of esoteric truths, and often find themselves years ahead of humanity's current understanding. Their role is to awaken remembrance through revelation.

Creators are the architects of the New Earth. While others interpret the world, Creators design it. They are encoded with vision and innovation, able to manifest new systems, structures, and paradigms aligned with higher consciousness. Creators may appear as artists, builders, engineers, leaders, or storytellers—but regardless of form, they are always bringing the invisible into the visible. Where others see brokenness, the Creator sees a blueprint waiting to be reborn. They operate beyond limitation, using their gifts to anchor divine possibilities into the physical world.

Mystics are the dimensional bridgers. They live between realms, moving in and out of spiritual frequencies with ease. Often guided by dreams, symbols, and intuitive knowing, Mystics bring direct connection to Source into human form. They experience visions, time distortions, astral travel, and contact with celestial beings.

Mystics are not limited by what can be explained—they carry what can only be experienced. Their presence reminds others that there is far more to reality than what meets the eye. They hold the vibration of the infinite.

Together, these three archetypes form a triad of divine embodiment: the Sage remembers, the Creator builds, and the Mystic reveals. And if you have felt ancient wisdom burn in your soul, a pull to make something new, or a life lived half between worlds—you may be one of them.

You didn't come here to follow the path.

You came here to map new ones into being.

All across the planet, they had arrived—the Avatars, the Chosen Ones—stationed with precision in every corner of the Earth. Among them, the most elite of all: the 144,000. Souls encoded with the highest activation frequencies, born not only to witness the shift—but to lead it. Each one placed with divine intent, woven into specific families, cultures, and timelines. Though veiled in forgetfulness, their inner codes remained untouched, quietly pulsing beneath the surface, awaiting the signal. The players were in position. The light was hidden in plain sight. And now... the Great Earth Mission was ready to begin.

Chapter 4: The Mission – Guardians of Humanity

Disrupting Systems of Illusion

The Chosen Ones did not come to bring war—they came to bring light. And in a world built on deception, light is the most disruptive force of all.

For far too long, humanity has been trapped in a carefully constructed illusion. Truth has been hidden. Knowledge suppressed. Systems of control—through religion, media, government, and false science—have shaped a reality that keeps people asleep. The masses walk in darkness, unaware of who they are, where they came from, or what they're capable of. Everything they've been taught has been designed to limit them.

The Chosen Ones were sent into this darkness to disrupt it from within.

They do not shout down the system—they reveal it. Their presence alone begins to loosen the false codes. Their insights trigger awakening. Their energy introduces something unfamiliar and powerful: remembrance.

They carry within them living frequencies that expose lies, challenge narratives, and break the spell of manipulation. When they speak, people remember things they never learned. When they enter a space, old energies begin to rise to the surface to be seen, cleared, and released.

They don't attack the old paradigm.

They outshine it.

Everywhere they go, they bring light into systems designed to conceal it. They raise the frequency, and in doing so, they dismantle the illusion from the inside out.

They are not here to adapt to this world.
They are here to remind it of the world that once was—
And the world that is coming.

Earth's Spiritual Imprisonment

A long time ago—before history as we know it—Earth was hijacked.
Fallen beings, once part of divine creation, deviated from their original purpose and turned against the cosmic order. They descended into lower densities and seized Earth, not as caretakers, but as tyrants. With cunning precision, they overthrew the natural spiritual currents of the planet and replaced them with something far more insidious: a planetary control system designed to trap the evolution of human consciousness. This system became what many now call the matrix—but it is more than a concept. It is a real, engineered energetic prison, a multidimensional web of distortion that overlays every aspect of Earth life. At its core, it was built to sever humanity's connection to Source, to keep souls bound in cycles of amnesia, limitation, and spiritual stagnation.
Religion, education, politics, entertainment, technology—these were not left untouched. Over time, they were infiltrated and repurposed to serve the illusion. The truth was not erased—it was buried beneath layers

of programming. Humanity was taught to forget, to fear, to obey. The soul's vast potential was hidden behind a veil so thick, most never realized they were even imprisoned.

This is not a metaphor.

Humanity has been enslaved and Earth, for thousands of years, has operated as a prison planet.

But prisons cannot hold the light forever.

The Chosen Ones were sent with a mission that transcends simple awakening. They came to infiltrate the matrix from within—to walk among the systems of control and begin to subtly unravel them. Their frequency destabilizes the false code. Their words, their presence, even their silence—carry the energy of truth. And truth is the one thing the matrix cannot sustain.

They are not here to revolt with violence or scream into the noise.

They are here to restore the natural order—to bring light where darkness took hold.

The spiritual war for Earth is real. It is ancient. And it is reaching its final phase.

These brave souls came to remind humanity of who they are, and to pierce the illusion that has been imposed upon them for millennia. Their mission is not easy. But it is clear:

To break the spell.

To shatter the prison.

To end the deception.

And when the time is right—

they will tear the false matrix apart, piece by piece, until nothing remains but light.

Reincarnation: Multiple Lifetimes for Mastery

Reincarnation is often spoken of as a sacred journey—a cycle of rebirth and evolution, where the soul returns again and again to learn, grow, and ultimately ascend.
But few realize the deeper truth:
Reincarnation, in its current form, was not part of the original divine plan.
It was never intended to be the primary path of ascension. Souls were meant to evolve through free will, divine memory, and direct connection to Source.

But after the dark forces seized control of Earth, they installed a closed loop system—a cycle of energetic entrapment that recycled souls endlessly through amnesia, pain, and limitation.
This system was designed to keep beings disempowered and disconnected.
Not to evolve them—but to control them.
And so, all souls who came to Earth—native or starborn—became bound to the loop. Even the highest light beings, those sent from celestial realms to help, became ensnared in the reincarnation grid. Their memories were stripped, their light veiled, and their missions delayed for lifetime after lifetime.
But still—they endured.

The Angelic-Human Hybrids, the Chosen Ones, came equipped with codes that the matrix could not fully suppress. Through each incarnation, they gathered

pieces of themselves, fragments of knowledge, sparks of memory. Each life was a sacred preparation, a chance to reclaim wisdom, strength, and soul mastery. What was meant to trap them became a crucible for their awakening.
They did not return by force—they returned by choice.
Not because they were powerless, but because their mission required mastery.
And through it all, something extraordinary happened:
They began to rise above it.

Lifetime by lifetime, they built strength. They broke old patterns. They remembered their origin. They activated ancient codes hidden deep within. And now, in this final age—the loop has no more power over them.
They have outgrown the prison.
Their frequency no longer matches the trap. Their consciousness no longer feeds it.

And with that, the illusion begins to break.
Ascension is no longer a distant goal—it is the next step.
The Chosen Ones have mastered the game. And now they are stepping beyond it.
This is the lifetime where they break the cycle.
This is the lifetime where they rise.
And this is how they ascend.

Preparing Humanity for Ascension

As the mission has progressed for the Chosen Ones, awakening themselves was only the beginning.

Their personal remembrance was never the end—it was the ignition. The moment they remembered who and what they truly were, a greater purpose was activated within them: to guide humanity out of darkness and into the light. For while they came to embody divine truth, they also came to share it. To be torches in the night. Beacons of a reality far more radiant than the one humanity has been taught to believe in.

They are not just here to awaken—they are here to awaken others.

With every thought, every action, every vibration they emit, they lift the frequency of the planet. Their words carry codes. Their energy realigns. Their presence alone causes distortion to unravel. And slowly, silently, without fanfare, they begin to shift the entire field of human consciousness.

They don't need to preach to teach.

They don't need to lead to lead.

Their very existence becomes the lesson. The reminder. The mirror.

Many walk among humanity completely unnoticed—yet wherever they go, change follows.

Others are more visible, carrying messages that stir the soul, that pierce the veil and awaken something long forgotten. Some heal. Some build. Some write. Some simply radiate. But all of them hold the light.

And now in 2025, the world is beginning to respond.

Humanity is awakening—rapidly, collectively, and in record numbers.

Souls are remembering who they are. Systems are crumbling. The veil is thinning. The Chosen Ones are not alone anymore—their presence is triggering a chain reaction that cannot be stopped.

And without them, Earth would remain in shadow.

They are the saviors foretold—not worshipped icons or distant messengers from the sky, but living, breathing souls walking beside you. They volunteered to descend into the darkness not to escape it, but to transform it. They are here to midwife the birth of a New Earth.

Every moment they embody their true frequency, they weaken the hold of the matrix.

Every heart they touch brings humanity one step closer to ascension.

Every truth they speak plants a seed that cannot be unremembered.

This is the divine responsibility they carry:

To remember, to rise, and to lead.

For in doing so, they bring the entire world with them.

Chapter 5: The God Code – The Divine Blueprint

Six-Stranded Divine DNA

Within the Angelic-Human Hybrids—the Chosen Ones—resides a hidden celestial architecture: a six-stranded DNA template, activated and encoded with divine intelligence. This is far more than biology. It is the sacred God Code—a multidimensional framework that links the body to higher planes of consciousness, memory, and universal light.

In the original divine design, all humans were intended to carry twelve active strands of DNA, each one corresponding to a dimensional layer of consciousness and spiritual function. These strands formed the full spectrum of what it meant to be a divine human: capable of love, wisdom, healing, telepathy, manifestation, and direct communion with Source.

But long ago, fallen angelic forces interfered. Through unauthorized genetic manipulation, they severed humanity's connection to higher dimensions by deactivating ten of these twelve strands. Native Earth humans, including Homo sapiens, were left with only two functional strands—just enough to sustain life, but far too little to access the full power of their divine potential.

The Chosen Ones were sent to change that.

Unlike the rest of the population, they were born with six active, bundled strands—a rare genetic structure inherited from celestial orders such as the 6D Indigo and Oraphim lineages.

These additional strands unlock higher sensory awareness, greater intuitive knowing, and access to interdimensional guidance and power.

More active DNA means more ability.

It means stronger energetic fields. Faster manifestation. Clearer insight. More light—because light is information, and DNA is the receiver. Each activated strand is a new antenna tuned to the frequencies of higher truth.

The primary work of The Chosen Ones is to awaken others.

Their presence acts as a trigger—a catalyst for DNA activation in those around them. Through their energy, their words, and their light, they begin to reawaken the dormant strands in humanity's genetic code. They carry within them the divine signal that tells others: "You are more than you've been told. You are more than you remember."

This is the heart of their mission.

To walk among the sleeping, and by simply being who they are—wake the world.

The fallen ones tried to erase the divine blueprint.

But the Chosen Ones are the proof that it still exists.

And now, that code is awakening once again.

Forbidden Knowledge Within DNA

Hidden deep within the DNA of the Chosen Ones lies more than celestial ancestry—it holds forbidden knowledge, encoded in light, waiting to be awakened. This is not myth or metaphor. It is living intelligence—divine memory—stored within their multidimensional genetic structure.

This knowledge includes the original design of the angelic human, the laws of universal creation, the mechanics of ascension, and the truth of Earth's manipulated history. It carries the understanding of how consciousness creates form, how energy shapes timelines, and how sound, frequency, and geometry birth worlds. It is knowledge that was once universally known—but has long been erased from public memory. And it has been withheld from humanity—suppressed by fallen forces that have ruled Earth through deception, illusion, and control. These powers severed the connection between humanity and its divine origin by disrupting their genetic blueprint.

The original divine human blueprint was built on a 12-strand DNA template, each strand corresponding to a higher level of dimensional awareness and spiritual power. Native Earth humans once carried this full potential, but ten of those strands were deactivated through manipulation, leaving most with only two functioning strands—enough to survive, but not enough to remember.

cultivated, every word is written for those who were sent here to alter the fate of Earth itself
This writing is not philosophy. This is encoded truth.
Not for the masses—but for the few.
The ones who chose themselves before they were ever chosen.

You will understand why your life has felt different. Why your path has been filled with events so extraordinary they defy logic. Why synchronicities surround you. Why you sense things others do not. You were not here to fit in—you were sent to activate. To disrupt the illusion. To raise the frequency of an entire planet. And you are not alone.

This book reveals the ancient laws that protect you. The powers that awaken in you. The abilities you were born to reclaim. The divine blueprint that was never lost—only waiting to be reawakened.

The chapters ahead will take you deep into the forgotten truths of your origin, your sovereign nature, your elite assignment, your divine protection, and your inevitable rise. You will come to understand that the real Great Awakening is not a global event—it is a personal one. It is you!

You are the prophecy.
You are the event.
And your time… is now.

This is the moment your soul has waited lifetimes for.

Open the pages.
Feel the activation.
Step into your remembrance.

Welcome, Chosen One.
The Universe has been waiting for you.

Chapter 1: Divine Incarnates – The Hidden Ones Unveiled

"For many are called, but few are chosen."

Ancient Texts

The Origins of the Chosen Ones in Sacred Traditions

Across the ages, sacred texts have whispered of rare and extraordinary beings—souls set apart by divine design, known as the Chosen Ones. Foretold in prophecy, their presence is woven into the fabric of ancient wisdom, spoken of as celestial emissaries who walk among humanity, protecting and guiding them toward the light.

When one hears the term "Chosen Ones," many minds immediately flash to ancient biblical prophecies—a distant memory of sacred texts, fiery sermons, and whispered legends of a mysterious number: the 144,000. While these ancient teachings do indeed contain seeds of truth, they represent only a small portion of a much greater and more profound story—a cosmic journey that spans beyond the pages of scripture into realms of infinite galaxies, celestial kingdoms, and divine destinies.

Throughout religious history, particularly in Christianity and Judaism, the number 144,000 has held great significance. In the Book of Revelation, it is said that exactly 144,000 souls—marked by divine intention and gathered from the 12 tribes of Earth—would rise as emissaries during Earth's final transformation. Esoteric traditions, too, have long spoken of this number, affirming it as a literal truth—a select group of souls, precisely numbered, called to lead humanity through its darkest times and into the dawn of a new era.

Yet, the true story of the "Chosen Ones" extends far beyond traditional religious teachings. These extraordinary beings are not confined to religious dogma or ancient interpretations. They are Angelic-Human Hybrids, cosmic royalty hidden in human form, sent from higher realms to walk the Earth at this pivotal moment in history. Their purpose transcends religious prophecy. Their true destiny is to awaken humanity and dismantle the systems of illusion that have kept it bound.

Indeed, the small number 144,000 out of 8 billion is accurate—a precise count marking these divine emissaries scattered across the planet. But their true purpose, their power, and their identity remain largely misunderstood by conventional teachings. They are not waiting for salvation; instead, they are the ones who will lead humanity into its greatest transformation. With their cosmic DNA, they carry the energy and wisdom of the universe itself. Their very presence is a living declaration of the universal awakening, shaking the foundations of outdated structures and heralding the birth of a new Earth.

This is not mere prophecy—this is cosmic destiny unfolding.

Welcome to the story of the real Chosen Ones—the hidden ones unveiled.

If you happen to be one of these rare and extraordinary beings, know this—this cosmic narrative is not just a story; it is your story. A profound realization awaits you, one that will shatter the illusions of limitation and reveal the boundless truth of who and what you truly are. This revelation extends far beyond the title of "Chosen One"—it is the key to unlocking a destiny greater than you have ever imagined.

Chosen vs Called – Clarifying Identity

The term "Chosen One" has long been used to describe those with a divine mission, but it carries a misleading implication—as if selection was based on favoritism rather than purpose. The truth is, you were not simply chosen—you were called.
Many were given the opportunity, but not all accepted. Out of a vast number of souls, only those with the strength, wisdom, and fortitude to endure this mission were selected. The path ahead was not easy, and many turned away. You were asked, and you chose to answer. That is the difference.

Why "Called" Is More Accurate Than "Chosen"
Being chosen suggests selection without choice, as if destiny was assigned to you without your participation.
Being called means you were invited based on your unique abilities and readiness—but you had to choose to step forward.
Many were given the chance, but only those prepared to endure the mission accepted.

Cosmic Origins of Angelic-Human Hybrids

These divine beings walk among humans, their celestial essence hidden beneath a mortal disguise. But they are not from here. Their true origin lies in realms beyond this world—vast luminous kingdoms governed by divine intelligence and higher law. They are not the result of Earth's evolutionary path.

The Chosen Ones are direct emanations from higher celestial orders, called forth to be present at this precise moment in Earth's unfolding. They are the 6D Indigos—radiant, ancient beings known in the higher realms as the Oraphim. What few understand is that these are not ordinary souls—they are incarnated extensions of their progenitors: the 12D Oraphim, supreme angelic forces and celestial architects of divine intelligence.

When the Earth timeline began to fall under distortion and interference from dark, fallen forces, the 12D Oraphim progenitors responded. To preserve the original divine template and assist in Earth's ascension, they created the 6D Indigo Oraphim—stepped down from their own celestial DNA yet still incredibly powerful. This elite race of angelic-human hybrids was not born of karma or evolutionary cycles, but of divine intention. They were designed as ground operatives—encoded with advanced DNA, multidimensional access, and the spiritual authority to override false systems and restore balance to the planetary grid.

The chosen ones are infused with the original blueprint of cosmic law. Their very energy carries the frequency of divine justice. Wherever they go, truth activates, illusion unravels, and the reality around them begins to shift. They are the celestial strike force sent from the heights of creation—to walk among humanity as catalysts of awakening and anchors of ascension.

These Angelic-Human Hybrids are not wanderers or seekers. They are not newly arrived souls discovering their place in the cosmos. They are veterans of creation, part of the original architects of light. Their role is not to blend into the background, but to subtly realign Earth's frequency with the divine pattern it was always meant to hold. The chosen ones are the most powerful beings on Planet Earth!

Other beings have also come—Starseeds, Lightworkers, and guides from across the stars. Each has their part to play. But the Chosen Ones stand in a category of their own—fewer in number, greater in purpose. They are not superior by hierarchy, but unique by design. They were not just sent to help. They were sent to lead the way forward and to completely destroy all darkness on Planet Earth!

Though Earth is not their native world, they have come to claim it. Not through conquest, but through restoration. Not through dominance, but through presence. Their origin is written in light, and their return was always prophesied. Earth may not be their home of birth—but it is their sacred inheritance.

Earth's Celestial Seeding

Long before recorded time, Earth was selected by celestial councils as the stage for a profound evolutionary design. This planet was infused with a sacred blueprint—a 12-strand DNA template capable of unlocking the full divine potential of the human form.

To carry out this divine program, two primary human lineages were seeded onto the planet:

1. Earthseeds – These were the original Root Races, evolving naturally through Earth's dimensional cycles. Their purpose was to activate the lower DNA strands (1–5) over time and experience. These became what we now call native humans.

2. Starseeds – Souls from higher realms who entered Earth's timeline carrying advanced spiritual architecture. Starseeds, including the few Chosen or Called Ones carrying a more specialized encoding and called for a unique mission, were seeded to safeguard

the full 12-strand divine template—particularly the dormant upper strands (6–12).

Although all appear human on the surface, their origins, function, and spiritual design differ greatly. Each was seeded with purpose—some to evolve through Earth, others to awaken it.

And yet, there is a third group—modern Homo sapiens—the dominant species on Earth today. While they were not part of the original celestial seeding plan, they are still part of the greater human family.

Their origin traces back to an unauthorized genetic experiment: a fusion of early Earth hominids with DNA from the fallen 11th-dimensional Annunaki. This interference disrupted the divine blueprint, deactivating ten of the twelve original DNA strands, leaving only two active by default.

But the story does not end there.

Though altered, Homo sapiens still carry the original 12-strand template buried deep within their morphogenetic field—and that template can be reactivated. The divine code is not lost, only dormant.

Now, in this great turning point of Earth's evolution, the Higher Councils of Light are working to restore and evolve the Homo sapiens lineage—guiding them back toward their divine potential, alongside the Earthseeds and Starseeds already in motion. The path may be different, but the destination is the same: ascension, sovereignty, and the reclamation of what was once hidden.

Humanity is not broken.
It is unfinished.
And now, the call to evolve is echoing across the stars.
This planet was originally seeded with greatness. And now, the ones who carry the ancient awakening codes are beginning to stir.
The awakening is no longer coming. It's already begun.

The Fall into Amnesia

Though the Chosen Ones originate from a high place in the cosmos—beginning in a royal and perfected state—they do not remember. That is the price of their descent into matter. The moment their soul crossed through the dimensional gates and entered the density of this realm, a great forgetting took place. The vast awareness they once carried—of who they are, where they came from, and why they came—was veiled behind a shroud of illusion.

This veil of amnesia was not a punishment. It was a divine agreement. To complete the mission, they had to walk among the sleeping as one of them. To awaken others, they first had to forget themselves. It is easy to carry the light in heaven—but to hold it in the darkness? That is the test of the Chosen.

From birth, there are signs—quiet, strange, unexplainable.

As children, they often felt isolated, watching the world as if behind glass. Family felt unfamiliar. School made little sense. They were often told they were "too sensitive," "too intense," or "too lost in their imagination." But deep inside, there was a presence—a quiet knowing that this world was not their true home.

They felt it in their dreams—so vivid, so real—flying, speaking with beings of light, standing in temples of crystal and gold. They felt it in the sadness that would hit them without cause. In the feeling of waiting for something... something big, something forgotten, something they couldn't explain.

Some remember staring at the stars, tears in their eyes, not knowing why.
Some felt déjà vu not as a glitch, but as a message—as if they had lived this before.
Some walked through life with an aching sense that something was missing—not from the world, but from themselves.

Many Starseeds, including Chosen Ones, have lived among native humans for so long they've taken on the shape of this world. They've absorbed its fears, its limitations, its false identities. They've forgotten their wings. They've mistaken the pain as their own, and the programming as truth. But the truth is—they are not one of them. They are here to help them.

The amnesia was necessary. It allowed the Chosen Ones to embed within the human story, to feel its weight, to know its struggle. But it was never meant to be permanent. Beneath the illusion, the memory still lives. Buried in the heart. Written in the soul. Programmed into the very cells of their body.

And now, the code is beginning to stir.

For those who came here to awaken—this is the moment before the remembering.
The veil is thinning.
The soul is rising.
And soon… the real story begins.

Chapter 2: The Choosing – Many Were Called

Who Chose the Chosen Ones?

This question has echoed across time: Who exactly chose the Chosen Ones?

Traditional teachings often present them as divinely favored—selected by grace, plucked from the crowd by an external god. But this concept is far too limited for the magnitude of the truth.

The Infinite Source plays no favorites. All souls are born of the same eternal spark. The Chosen Ones were not lifted above others—they rose. They were not gifted their roles—they claimed them.

These beings are warriors of light, guardians of sacred truth, emissaries of celestial law. Their arrival on Earth was no accident. Each incarnation was orchestrated with precision. Each life, placed with intention.

And though they were sent… they volunteered. In a higher realm, before time unfolded, they stepped forward. They said yes to the mission others turned away from. They accepted the burden few could carry.

In that sense—they chose themselves. And because of that, they were chosen.

The 144,000 were not selected out of favoritism—but out of fortitude. They were called because they had the resilience, the awareness, and the power to shift the fate of a world. Not to be worshipped. Not to be elevated. But to serve, awaken, and liberate.

So who chose them?

Selection by the Highest Order

We tell you the truth—many were called, but only a few were brave enough to answer.

A long time ago, a heartfelt cry was heard in the highest heavens—a cry from Earth.

It rose as a signal of pure soul energy, sent out from a planet drowning in illusion. Humanity had become lost, disconnected from its divine origin, slipping deeper into distortion. The cry was felt across the stars—and the cosmos responded.

In the higher realms, the Sirian High Council received this distress call and they gathered in concern. These were sixth-dimensional architects of evolution—elders and guardians of light. With them stood the Council of Light, the Archangels, and the Supreme Guardians of the Multiverse. Together, they formed a sacred alliance to initiate what would become one of the greatest missions in the cosmos.

The Calling

This High council sent a great call out across the cosmos for elite beings to go to Earth to help humanity.

This call was not heard with ears, but felt deep within the soul. A frequency moved across galaxies, summoning the most ancient and advanced beings—Starseeds, Indigos, Oraphim. They remembered. They came forward. They volunteered to descend into density, to forget who they were, to awaken from within the illusion.

But offering to serve was not enough.

This mission would require total surrender. It would mean giving up everything—divine memory, comfort, certainty. It meant experiencing betrayal, loss, and isolation in a world that would not recognize them. And even among the willing, not all were ready.

Among those who responded were the 6D Indigos—the Oraphim—beings carrying the original divine blueprint. To them the councils asked:

"Who will go down to Earth?"

And for a moment… all was still.

The thought of descending into such darkness shook even the strongest among them. To lower their frequency so far, to be stripped of memory, to enter a world so deeply veiled in illusion—many could not bear it. Some stepped back.

But not all.

You stepped forward.

You were not forced. You were not randomly assigned.

You were called—and in a sense, you chose yourself. You were brave enough to answer.

Your soul was examined. Your coding confirmed. Your light was steady. You had endured fire in other worlds and carried the scars of service. You knew the cost. And still—you said yes.

From the billions who were called, only a few were chosen. Not as favorites, but as the most prepared. The most anchored. The most resilient.

And now, you are here.

Not by chance.

You were called—and you chose to remember.
And in that choice... you became one of the Chosen.

Soul Contracts and Agreements

Before your feet ever touched the Earth, before your first breath was drawn in this human form, an ancient agreement was made.

You didn't simply show up here unprepared—you came with intention, with purpose, and with a sacred blueprint etched into your very soul. There was a contract... but it was not imposed upon you. You helped write it.

In the higher realms, surrounded by light and clarity, you saw what Earth was. You saw the darkness, the distortion, the chaos. You saw the beauty too. And in that space of divine awareness, you made a decision: you would go.

With the guidance of celestial mentors—members of the Sirian High Council, the Council of Light, and your own soul family—you began to design the intricate map of your Earthly incarnations. Every major turning point, every challenge, every moment of pain and breakthrough, was chosen with precision.

You didn't choose ease. You chose growth.
You didn't choose perfection. You chose contrast.
You chose to fall so you could rise.

You crafted each lifetime around lessons you wished to master, people you would meet, souls you would love, and betrayals you would endure. You selected your family, your body, your name—even the wounds you would carry, knowing they would become portals to your awakening.

Most importantly, you agreed to forget.

You agreed to walk through the illusion blind, disconnected from the truth of who you are—just to see if you could remember.

This was not punishment. This was power.
Because in remembering… you reclaim it all.

These soul contracts were not random assignments handed down by distant deities. They were personal, deliberate, sacred. You signed them in full awareness of the density you would face—because you also knew the light you carried could transform it.

You understood that Earth would not change by force, but by frequency.
So you chose to become the frequency.

This is what it means to be a Chosen One.
Not chosen in privilege, but in participation.
Not bound by fate, but empowered by choice.

And now, that contract is beginning to activate.
Every struggle has led you to this page.
Every hardship has carved the vessel that carries your light.
And everything you planned is already unfolding.

lite Angelic Training

Once your soul contract was complete and every detail of your Earth mission had been carefully designed, you entered a sacred phase of preparation—a divine training unlike anything in this universe. In realms of radiant intelligence and perfect harmony, you trained with master beings—elders, ascended architects, and celestial guardians—who poured their wisdom into you. You were shown how to hold light in the darkest realms, how to remember truth in the face of illusion, and how to move energy with thought alone. These weren't lessons in theory—they were initiations of soul. You became a master being long before you ever arrived here. Not by title, but by experience. And when your training was complete, you were not cast out—you were honored. You were sent. Not because you were ready to be served, but because you were finally ready to serve.

The Descent to Earth

And then the moment came. A stillness swept across the higher realms as the chosen gathered at the threshold of time. The plans were complete. The codes within us were set. Earth's cry had been heard—and now, it was time to answer.

With one final breath, we stepped forward—

And leapt.

We plunged into the portal between worlds, falling from brilliance into shadow, from boundless light into the narrowing corridors of density. As we descended, we passed through realm after realm, each one heavier, slower, more distorted than the last.

And with every level we fell, we felt it—
The pain.
The compression.
The sharp burn of separation.
The ache of forgetting.
What was once effortless became struggle. What was once whole began to fracture.
Until finally...
We reached the final gate—
And crossed through the sacred veil of birth.
Born into flesh. Wrapped in amnesia. Eyes open, yet blind to who we were.
But even in that moment—somewhere deep within—we still carried the code.
We had arrived.
The mission had begun.

The Chosen Ones, however, carry a rare inheritance. They were born with a six-stranded active template, passed down through the Oraphim and 6D Indigo lineages—a specialized version of the Emerald Order. These six active strands are bundled with the dormant codes of the full 12-strand system, allowing them to unlock advanced awareness, powerful abilities, and direct access to divine memory.

This is how they carry within them the Emerald Founder Records—the most sacred body of cosmic knowledge in existence. These records, safeguarded in higher dimensions by the Emerald Order, were encoded directly into the DNA of the Oraphim and their Earth representatives. Once activated, the Chosen Ones don't learn this knowledge—they remember it. It rises spontaneously through frequency, awakening visions, knowing, and purpose.

This is why the dark ones fear them.
Not because they rebel.
But because they remember.
Their very presence is a threat to the matrix of illusion.
Because as they awaken, so does the truth.
And once the forbidden knowledge returns to Earth—nothing can ever be the same.

Threats from Controlling Powers

The world you see around you—governments, media, institutions, and religious systems—was not built to support your awakening. It was built to prevent it.

For centuries, hidden behind polished pulpits, political podiums, and powerful corporate systems, a silent war has been waged—not on nations, but on consciousness. The awakening of Angelic-Human Hybrids—those carrying the divine code and forbidden knowledge—represents the single greatest threat to the systems of control that rule this planet.

Why?

Because an awakened Chosen One cannot be controlled.

They cannot be lied to. They cannot be manipulated. They see through illusion. They dismantle programming. Their very frequency destabilizes artificial systems built on fear, hierarchy, and deception.

And so, the powers that be—governments, shadow institutions, elite cabals, and religious hierarchies—have always feared their return.

They have implemented secret surveillance, disinformation campaigns, targeted spiritual attacks, and programs designed to label, isolate, and suppress awakening souls. From false diagnoses to chemical sedatives, from staged events to distorted doctrines—every effort has been made to keep the Chosen Ones asleep or confused about who they really are.

Why such effort? Why such fear?

Because the Chosen Ones carry within them the light that shatters the matrix.
And not just symbolically—literally.
Their DNA disrupts frequency fences. Their thoughts collapse illusions. Their energy restores memory in others. They carry the blueprints of divine truth—truth that threatens to unravel every lie that holds the old system together.
The fallen forces know this. The governments they influence know this.
And that is why you've been made to feel "too much," "too different," or "too broken."
You were never broken. You were dangerous—to them.
And now, their time is running out.
Because no force, no matter how dark, can stop the light from remembering itself.
And you, Chosen One, are the living memory of that light.

Chapter 6: Superhuman Abilities – Power of the Gods

Psychic and Intuitive Mastery

Awakened Angelic-Human Hybrids possess abilities that stretch far beyond what the world considers normal. These are not learned skills—they are ancient powers encoded into their DNA, activated through remembrance and awakening. As their vibration rises and their dormant strands ignite, they begin to access what can only be described as superhuman abilities—gifts that once defined the gods.

Among the most prominent of these are their psychic and intuitive capacities, which awaken first. These are the subtle senses that defy logic but ring with truth.

They experience hyper-intuition, an unshakable inner knowing that reveals truths before they're spoken. They simply know—when someone is lying, when something is about to happen, when energy shifts around them. This knowing, known as claircognizance, operates like a spiritual download: sudden bursts of wisdom with no source other than the soul.

Their empathic sensitivity is equally profound. They don't just read emotions—they feel them, as if they were their own. When near others, they absorb vibrations, sometimes feeling overwhelmed in crowds or drained by negativity. But with mastery, this gift becomes a precision instrument for healing, guidance, and deep energetic alignment.

They are sensitive to thoughts, frequencies, and unseen energies. Many hear subtle guidance from their higher selves or celestial guides. They feel when timelines shift. They sense changes in collective consciousness. They are living antennas—transmitters and receivers of universal truth.

Examples are everywhere:

A Chosen One senses a loved one is in danger hours before a call arrives.

Another walks into a room and instantly knows who's hiding pain behind a smile.

One receives an image or phrase during meditation, only to find it manifest physically days later.

Another hears a silent voice urging them to change course, only to avoid disaster by moments.

These are not coincidences.

This is what happens when cosmic memory reactivates.

When divine intelligence flows through a human vessel.

These gifts are not fantasy. They are the natural state of a fully awakened being—

and they are just the beginning.

Elemental and Natural Control

Beyond their intuitive and psychic mastery, awakened Angelic-Human Hybrids possess an even more mysterious and awe-inspiring gift—the ability to influence and harmonize with the elemental forces of nature. This is not folklore or myth. It is a natural extension of their cosmic design.

Because they are deeply encoded with the original frequencies of divine creation, they possess an inherent energetic link to the elemental kingdom—earth, air, fire, water, and ether. Their presence alone, when activated, can subtly shift natural environments, bringing balance, movement, or even disruption depending on the frequency they emit.

Some Angelic-humans report the ability to calm storms with their intentions, calling on peace and stillness to settle violent skies. Others find that animals are drawn to them, sensing the purity of their frequency. Some witness weather patterns shift around them during moments of heightened emotion or focused prayer—rain stopping mid-step, wind responding to their energy, or lightning flashing in affirmation.

These are not illusions.

They are resonant exchanges between a multidimensional being and a conscious universe.

Because everything in creation is alive. The wind listens. The trees remember. The water responds. And when a Chosen One moves into alignment with their higher self, the natural world recognizes them—not as an outsider, but as one of its architects.

Examples are powerful and often unforgettable:

A Chosen One walking in silence suddenly watches a flock of birds spiral above them in a perfect circle, mirroring their emotions.

Another sits in quiet meditation, and the winds rise without warning, swirling around them like a protective cocoon.

One calls for clarity in the middle of a storm, and the skies part—sunlight piercing through dense clouds moments later.

Others feel the energy of ancient trees, receiving messages through vibration and intuition.
These aren't tricks of the mind. They are signs of restored harmony—a being once again in communion with creation.
This elemental connection is not about domination.
It's about resonance. Alignment. Cooperation.
It is divine authority expressed through humility and harmony.
And it is one more reminder that the Chosen Ones are not bound by the rules of this world—
They were sent to rewrite them.

Interdimensional Communication

Once the Chosen Ones awaken to their true nature, a gateway opens within them—an energetic bridge linking Earth to the higher realms. Through this bridge, they begin to access something few on Earth remember: interdimensional communication.
This gift allows Angelic-Human Hybrids to communicate telepathically with celestial intelligences, ascended masters, angelic beings, and members of their own soul councils. The conversations are not spoken aloud—they are felt, known, seen, and heard in the quiet of the inner world. These transmissions arrive as direct downloads,

symbols, tones, visions, or entire blocks of knowing that bypass language altogether.
These messages often come in meditation, during sleep, or spontaneously in moments of stillness. Some receive them as clear voices.

Others as sudden clarity that seems to emerge from nowhere. But all who activate this ability recognize the presence of something greater reaching through the veil to deliver guidance, warning, or confirmation.
Because Chosen Ones originate from higher dimensions, they are born with the energetic architecture needed to access them again. Their DNA—especially the higher dormant strands—acts like a cosmic antenna, tuning them into frequencies far beyond the range of ordinary perception.
Through this tuning, they are able to:
Bridge multiple realities at once, seeing layers of truth within a moment others would miss.
Receive direct wisdom from higher realms without relying on physical teachers or texts.
Communicate across time and space, connecting with future or past versions of themselves, or assisting others through the astral and etheric planes.
Sense dimensional shifts, knowing when a timeline is changing or when unseen forces are at play.
Many Chosen Ones are contacted by their galactic families, their councils of light, or the original architects of the divine plan. These communications are rarely dramatic, but always profound—filled with peace, love, and the unmistakable signature of cosmic truth.
They begin to realize:

They are never alone.
They never have been.
Their guides have walked beside them since the beginning, waiting only for their vibration to rise high enough to hear the call. And once the call is heard, the communication never stops.

This is more than channeling.
This is remembrance.
This is cosmic reunion through the inner technology of divine DNA.
And it is a power only the awakened can fully wield.

Quantum Reality Manipulation

Perhaps the most extraordinary ability awakened Angelic-Human Hybrids begin to access is the power of conscious reality manipulation—a mastery of energy, frequency, and intention that enables them to shift timelines, rewrite outcomes, and reshape their experience of reality itself.
This isn't fiction.
It's quantum law.
The universe does not respond to effort—it responds to vibration. And when a Chosen One raises their frequency to align with their divine nature, reality begins to respond to them like a mirror—reflecting their inner state outward in amplified form.
This is the essence of quantum reality manipulation:

They are no longer subject to the world around them—they begin to shape it.

They intuitively understand that time is not linear, but fluid. With heightened awareness, they begin to move between possible timelines, sensing what's ahead and choosing the path aligned with their highest outcome. Some experience this as déjà vu, prophetic insight, or sudden redirection. Others witness events shift almost instantly based on a change in thought, emotion, or energy.

Through this mastery, they can:

Quantum jump—shifting from one probable timeline to another with focused intention and vibrational precision.

Collapse negative outcomes before they manifest by refusing to feed them energetically.

Bend time—experiencing accelerations, slowdowns, or distortions of linear time during moments of heightened consciousness.

Manifest synchronicities, events, and outcomes seemingly out of thin air, through alignment rather than effort.

Surrounding them is a powerful energetic field, a living aura encoded with divine intelligence. When activated, this field becomes a magnetic shield—attracting high-frequency experiences, people, and opportunities, while repelling lower-vibrational energies that no longer match their frequency.

Negative people, toxic situations, and dark forces simply cannot remain in their presence for long. Their very vibration disrupts falsehood, dissolves interference, and clears space for truth to reign.

This is not magic.

It is mastery.

It is the result of divine technology encoded within their DNA—now reactivated and fully online.

And this power is not meant to control others.

It is meant to anchor light into the fabric of Earth's reality, shifting the collective matrix by living as a bridge between heaven and Earth.

The Chosen Ones are walking quantum fields—living proof that consciousness creates reality.

And as they fully awaken to this, the old world will fall, and a new one will rise.

Chapter 7: Divine Synchronicity – Guided by Fate

The Language of the Universe

The Universe speaks—but not in words.

It speaks in patterns. In symbols. In frequencies. It weaves messages through numbers, dreams, timing, signs, and energy. And for the Chosen Ones—those born into divine mission—this language is not just noticed... it is lived.

These are not coincidences. Not accidents. Not random flickers in a meaningless world.
They are angelic transmissions, cosmic whispers, divine nudges delivered through the fabric of reality itself.
They are the sacred conversation between Source and soul—alive, intelligent, and ongoing.

A string of numbers appears again and again—11:11, 144, 777—as if the Universe itself is echoing something deep and ancient.
A butterfly floats into view during a moment of inner turmoil.
A feather falls at your feet as you question your next step.
A book opens to the exact line you needed.
A billboard flashes a single word that strikes like lightning in your heart.

To most people, these moments pass unseen.
But for the Chosen Ones—they are unmistakable.
They are messages. Markers. Confirmations from beyond the veil.

Each carries frequency. Each is tailored to your energy in that precise moment. Each is a signal that something greater is unfolding—even if you can't yet see the full picture.

And the more aligned you become, the more this language floods your life.

The Universe speaks in number codes:

11:11 – Awakening. A call to presence. Alignment unfolding.
222 – Harmony. Relationships. The power of duality and unity.
333 – Divine support. Ascended masters guiding you.
444 – Protection. You are surrounded by light.
555 – Transformation. Let go—change is here.
666 – Refocus. Return to your center. Adjust your vibration.
777 – Divine flow. Spiritual mastery. Synchronic magic.
888 – Power, abundance, infinite energy cycles.
999 – Completion. Graduation of a soul lesson.
144 – Activation. The DNA code of the Chosen Ones.

But numbers are only one dialect.

The Universe also speaks through signs—physical, literal, symbolic.

A white feather appears on a dark sidewalk.
A butterfly crosses your path not once, but three times in a day.
You overhear the same phrase from three different strangers.
A symbol keeps appearing—on walls, in dreams, on the side of a truck.
A scent reminds you of something you've never consciously known.
You walk into a space and feel... something. A presence. A vibration.
It's all part of the message.

Even glitches in technology, repeated names, unexpected animals crossing your path, or words highlighted over and over in random places—they are codes in the matrix, flashing behind the illusion, asking you to notice... to listen... to follow.

These are not simply comforts.
They are confirmations.
And they do not come when nothing is happening.
They come because something is already in motion.

The more aligned the Chosen One becomes, the more fluent this language grows.

Synchronicity becomes a rhythm.
Signs become strategy.
Guidance becomes conversation.

You no longer ask, "Is this real?"
You feel it. You know.

Because for the Chosen Ones, the Universe doesn't just whisper—it roars in divine precision.
It rearranges your reality.
It codes your path.
It lights your way.

There is no such thing as coincidence. There never was. Everything is message. Everything is meaning. Everything is divine.

And once you begin to listen, really listen,
You awaken the gift hidden in plain sight:

The ability to speak—and live—
in the Language of the Universe.

Understanding Synchronicities

There comes a moment in the journey of every Chosen One when reality begins to shimmer—when the veil thins, and a hidden rhythm emerges beneath the surface of ordinary life.

For them, synchronicity is not a rare phenomenon—it is a constant hum beneath the timeline, a celestial intelligence weaving moments together in real time. These moments are more than coincidences. They are precise calibrations from a higher realm—signals encoded in the unfolding of time and space, designed specifically for the Chosen Ones.

11:11 on the clock—again.
A butterfly crosses their path just as they ask for a sign.
A stranger speaks a phrase that matches the dream from the night before.
A song on the radio answers a silent question in their mind.

At first, these patterns may seem random... surreal. But over time, a deeper knowing arises. The Chosen One begins to sense the energy behind these alignments. They feel the message in their bones. And they begin to recognize what others cannot see: these are not chance events. These are divine instructions—breadcrumbs scattered by the Universe across their path.

What makes the Chosen Ones different is not simply that synchronicities occur more often—it's that they are conscious of them. Hyper-aware. Tuned in. They listen. They feel. They respond. They follow the signs like sacred coordinates guiding them toward destiny.

Eventually, they realize: they've been communicating with the Universe all along. And now, the Universe is answering back.

This conversation builds. The more they notice the signs, the more frequently they appear. One message leads to another. A symbol links to a memory. A person says something that connects to a past vision—and suddenly, everything aligns. What was once hidden becomes obvious. The sequence was there all along.

Sometimes a painful event from years ago—something once dismissed as meaningless—suddenly reveals itself as a pivotal turning point. A loss becomes a redirection. A missed opportunity opens the exact door they needed. A moment of heartbreak becomes the spark that ignited their awakening.

These are not random accidents. These are the mechanics of synchronicity at work.

And in the lives of the Chosen Ones, they are constant.

A person they met for only five minutes shifts the entire trajectory of their life. A decision made on a whim turns out to be a soul contract unfolding. A place they were never supposed to go becomes the stage for their greatest transformation.

Each sign, each alignment, is a holy thread in a larger tapestry that only reveals its full image in hindsight.

Synchronicities are not just signs. They are revelations. They are divine machinery in motion—cosmic gears turning quietly behind the scenes, adjusting the Chosen One's path in real time.

This is how the Universe guides them—not through instruction, but through intuition. Not through control, but through alignment. The signs do not force movement—they invite it. They do not demand obedience—they awaken remembrance.

Eventually, the Chosen One stops asking, "Is this a sign?"

They know.

They feel it.

Synchronicity becomes the language they live by.

This language is not vague or symbolic. It is deeply personal, precisely tuned, and always timed with perfection. It's a sacred dance between their soul and the cosmos—one that becomes more fluid the more they surrender to its rhythm.

And the deeper truth is this:

These signs are not trying to comfort them.
They are trying to activate them.
To wake them up.
To remind them of the mission they came here to complete.
To call them back into alignment with the timeline of their highest purpose.

This is the orchestration guiding every true Chosen One.
It is not random.
It is not subtle.
It is divine intelligence in motion—coded events, sent across time, designed to awaken them, guide them, and launch them into destiny.

Look closely. Listen deeply.

The Universe is speaking.
And it always has been.

Timelines and Alignment: The Path They Were Meant to Walk

For the Chosen Ones, every synchronicity is more than a sign. It is an echo from a higher timeline—a pulse from their soul's original blueprint, reminding them of the path they came here to walk.

Time is not a straight line for these beings. It is layered, bending, alive. Every moment of awareness, every choice, every energy shift moves them closer to—or further from—the divine trajectory mapped before birth.

There is a sacred path, etched in light. A current of destiny where their mission aligns effortlessly. On this path, the right people appear at the right moment. Events unfold without force. Doors open without resistance. Miracles move freely, and synchronicities flow like breath. But this path cannot be forced. It must be felt.

The Universe guides them like a living compass. When they drift, the current slows. Signs grow quiet. Friction increases. Flow gives way to heaviness. But when they return to alignment—when their frequency rises back into resonance—the signs flood in like thunder. Reality begins to respond instantly.

A five-second delay... and they sidestep disaster.
A wrong turn... and they find a revelation.
A rejection... becomes divine redirection.
A collapse... becomes resurrection.

And sometimes, when the Chosen Ones drift too far from their intended path, the Universe will intervene—powerfully and without apology. It dismantles what no longer serves. It removes what cannot follow. It resets the course completely. What appears to be chaos is often sacred correction. A timeline snapping back into place.

They may not see it right away. They may feel pain, confusion, even loss. But in time, they understand: something higher was steering them. Something holy was working behind the scenes.

There is a version of their life where their power is unlocked, their gifts activated, and their mission fulfilled. That timeline is real. It already exists. And the Universe is doing everything it can to lead them there.

The more they trust, the more it unfolds. The more they align, the faster destiny accelerates.
And through it all, one truth remains:

They are never walking alone.
The Universe is walking with them.
Step by step.
Sign by sign.
Breath by divine breath.

Chapter 8: Trials by Fire – Angelic Strength

Enduring Spiritual Attacks

To be a Chosen One is to shine with a light so radiant, so unshakably pure, that it disrupts the darkness wherever it appears. But make no mistake—**that light draws fire.** The brighter the soul, the more it is targeted.

From the moment they incarnate, Angelic-Human hybrids are marked—not just by divine forces, but by the opposition. They enter the battlefield of Earth already known by name in the unseen realms. And because they are here to dismantle illusion and collapse the false matrix, they are met with resistance at every level.

The attacks don't always come as visible enemies. More often, they come silently, invisibly—psychic warfare that strikes at the mind, emotional sabotage that isolates the heart, energetic interference that throws them off course. These beings feel everything. And the darker forces know it.

They are tested constantly.

False friends appear—only to betray them.
Family turns cold, unable to understand their frequency.
Workplaces become arenas of resistance.
Random strangers lash out for no reason.

Sleep becomes a battlefield.
Their minds become war zones.
Their bodies carry wounds no doctor can diagnose.

Why? Because they pose a threat. A real one.

These are not ordinary souls. They carry codes in their DNA that can awaken others. They destabilize illusions simply by existing. Their very presence begins to unravel the old programs embedded in this world. And that is something the darkness cannot allow without a fight.

Emotional isolation becomes a way of life. They feel alien—misunderstood, too deep, too intense, too sensitive. But these are not flaws. These are indicators of who they are: *cosmic insurgents hiding in human skin.*

The attacks are designed to break their spirit—to distract, discourage, and destroy before their mission activates fully. The enemy knows they are powerful. The tests intensify the closer they get to unlocking their gifts.

People around them may suddenly change—behaving strangely, turning hostile, speaking words that seem loaded with venom or confusion. These are not always personal attacks. **They are manipulations.** Dark energies use others as vessels to get close, to weaken resolve, to twist perception. This is psychic interference at its most dangerous: invisible, subtle, and strategic.

But through it all, the Chosen Ones rise.

Each betrayal becomes a sharpening.
Each heartbreak becomes a lesson in discernment.
Each attack becomes another reason to stand taller.
Each tear becomes a purification of power.

They learn to hold their light steady in the storm.
They learn to see through illusion.
They learn to listen to the energy behind the words.
And most of all, they learn who they really are.

This fire was never meant to destroy them. It was meant to *forge* them.

They are not victims. They are not weak.
They are being tempered into living weapons of light—
beings who cannot be moved, silenced, or broken.

This is the price of awakening.
This is the path of the Chosen Ones.

And though it burns—it also transforms.
Because from these ashes, something greater rises.

A force that darkness cannot touch.
A soul it cannot deceive.
A being it cannot stop.

This is angelic strength.
Born of trials.
Refined by fire.
Unleashed by mission.
And destined… to change the world.

Emotional and Relational Challenges

From the very beginning, most Chosen Ones are born into families that feel off. The energy doesn't match. The love feels conditional, if present at all. And the deeper reason is this: many are placed into human families not to find comfort but to ignite awakening. The home becomes the first battleground. And the battlefield is emotional.

It's not always physical abuse, though for some it is. More often, it's the deep psychic wound of never being seen. Of being silenced, ridiculed, dismissed.

Often, there is one dominant personality—a narcissist, a control figure, a shadow agent—who seems to exist solely to break them. These figures, knowingly or not, are placed there by darker forces to try and dominate the light of the Chosen One before it fully awakens.

But here is the paradox: every attempt to destroy them only makes them stronger.

The Chosen Ones are tested through the crucible of emotional pain. Betrayal is common. Rejection by those they love most is almost inevitable. They grow up carrying questions they can't put into words. Why do I feel so different? Why don't they love me the way I love them? Why does my presence seem to trigger others?

At first, this pain runs deep. Before their awakening, many Chosen Ones internalize the hurt and begin to ask, what's wrong with me? The emotional wounds can stretch across years, even decades. And yet, this suffering is not without meaning. Through it, they develop a sacred strength—a spiritual resilience unmatched by anything the world can throw at them.

Eventually, a revelation breaks through the sorrow.

There was never anything wrong with them. They were simply surrounded by people who could not comprehend their energy, their brilliance, their purpose.

In truth, these emotional battles are the pre-initiation—the first fires that forge the soul into divine steel.

They begin to realize they were never unloved. They were simply placed in the presence of those who couldn't love beyond ego. They were never broken. They were surrounded by people who were terrified of their light. They were never meant to fit in. They were born to stand apart and light the way.

Remember this: many Chosen Ones have lived among humans for so long, they begin to believe they are one of them. But they are not. They came here for the humans, not from them. Even after the abuse, the pain, the exile—they return again and again to uplift, protect, and awaken the very ones who tried to bury them.

It's the ultimate act of divine love.

But this journey isn't just about families. It extends to every kind of relationship—friendships that turn sour, mentors who betray, lovers who deceive. The Chosen Ones attract intensity because their energy amplifies everything. What is hidden in others is exposed in their presence. What is false falls apart. Their light demands authenticity—and most can't handle it.

Romantic relationships are often the most painful. They love with a depth and purity that overwhelms ordinary hearts. They are devoted, intuitive, and empathic—but also magnetically intense. And that intensity either heals or exposes. Early romantic connections are frequently karmic, filled with lessons, illusions, and heartbreak. But these, too, serve the path.

Because after the illusions fall, the real one comes.

Usually later in life, the Chosen One is led to a true counterpart. A stabilizing mirror. A partner who understands their mission, honors their energy, and brings balance to their journey. This is the real Twin Flame—not a fantasy born of longing, but a union forged in the fire of spiritual growth. And it only arrives when both have done the inner work.

It is part of the path. And it was always part of the plan.

Through it all, the Chosen Ones discover the most important love of all: the love of Source within. It fills every wound. It replaces every betrayal. It becomes so radiant, so complete, that external validation no longer holds power. They realize they were never truly unloved, because they are and always have been the embodiment of love itself.

So to every Chosen One who has felt alone. To every one of you who has been betrayed, abandoned, silenced, and shamed.

Know this. Your isolation was never punishment. It was refinement.

And when the grand awakening comes, you will see clearly why it all had to happen. You will be healed. You will be restored. And you will embrace what you once feared the most. That being different is the greatest blessing in the entire universe.

Purpose of Adversity

Adversity is the sacred forge through which the Chosen Ones are transformed. Every trial, every storm, every unexpected twist in their path is part of a greater orchestration—designed to awaken the greatness encoded deep within them.

Every Chosen One carries a radiant energy—so refined, so potent—that it must be revealed under pressure. The intensity of this world becomes the fire that tempers their light into unshakable power. These are not just difficult experiences—they are initiations. And with each one, something greater is activated within.

They are refined like master blades—through fire, through friction, through the sacred process of becoming. Like elite celestial warriors undergoing the most advanced special forces training, they are prepared through discipline, challenge, and endurance. Their character is fortified. Their inner light is strengthened. And their spiritual armor is forged in truth.

Each challenge peels away another layer of limitation. Each emotional blow carves away illusion. Every disappointment, every betrayal, every delay—all of it pushes them closer to the core of who they really are. These trials are not punishment. They are precision-guided awakenings.

From the outside, their lives may look like chaos. But beneath the surface, something magnificent is unfolding. The soul of the Chosen One is being summoned into remembrance. Their codes are activating. Their destiny is aligning.

These experiences are designed to build qualities that no classroom can teach: divine patience, cosmic humility, unshakable compassion, and the strength to walk through fire without being burned. The soul is not being broken—it is being revealed.

And when the Chosen One reaches that moment—when the fire has done its work and the codes of identity burst open from within—it becomes one of the most powerful events in the cosmos.

The awakening of the Chosen One unleashes a light so powerful it reaches the heavens. A frequency so pure, so unstoppable, it realigns destinies. It shifts timelines. It accelerates the evolution of Earth itself.

This is the purpose of adversity. Not to test. Not to destroy. But to call forth the divine within.

To reveal the unstoppable, eternal being the Chosen One was always meant to be.

Chapter 9: The Protected Ones – Touch Them Not

Cosmic Protection Laws

There exists in the higher realms a sacred law that governs all existence—an unshakable command woven into the very fabric of creation. It is known simply as the One Law, and it says: Do no harm.

All benevolent divine beings honor this law. It is not just a rule—it is the essence of balance, the code of universal sovereignty. And when this law is kept, all other divine laws fall into alignment. This single truth becomes the cornerstone of all spiritual order.

This is a free will universe. Every being, from the highest angel to the darkest fallen entity, has the power to choose. Even the power to harm. But free will comes with a caveat—a cosmic accountability that cannot be bypassed.

For harm to occur, there must be consent. Permission. An energetic agreement—whether conscious or unconscious. This is where deception enters the equation.

Fallen beings and lower entities exploit what is called implied consent. If you do not say "no," they twist it into a "yes." If you remain unaware, they claim permission by default. If you are ignorant of your right to reject interference, they move in.

This is why awareness is protection. And why the word "no" is among the most powerful spiritual defenses in existence. To stand in your sovereignty and say no—to contracts, to interference, to energies not aligned with your mission—is to activate the built-in shields of divine law.

For the average human soul, learning to say no is a vital step toward spiritual protection. It sets boundaries and revokes permission from harmful forces operating in this realm of free will. But for the Chosen Ones, it goes deeper.

Before awakening, even they must consciously deny consent—saying no to interference, manipulation, and energetic intrusion. But once awakened, something profound shifts. Protection becomes automatic. Sovereignty becomes encoded.

Their very essence begins to radiate a frequency that rejects anything unaligned. They no longer need to speak it—their presence says it for them. Saying no is no longer just a decision—it becomes a way of being. They don't just set boundaries—they *are* the boundary. Their awakened energy field is impenetrable. Their DNA broadcasts divine authority.

They don't ask for protection—they are protected.

This divine immunity is not arrogance—it is earned through lifetimes of service and coded through cosmic design. The Chosen Ones are not like the rest. They carry light that disrupts the lower realms, and as such, they are prime targets for spiritual opposition. But the universe anticipated this—and installed safeguards that ensure they cannot be taken down by dark forces.

Those who attempt to harm a Chosen One step into a spiritual trap of their own making. The repercussions are swift and undeniable. Not because the Chosen One retaliates—but because the universe itself moves to restore balance.

This is divine justice. An equal energetic return—a balancing of all things.

What many call karma is not punishment. It is cause and effect on a cosmic scale. And in the case of harming a Chosen One, the energetic weight is far heavier—because the light they carry is exponentially greater. Interfering with that light does not just delay an individual—it threatens the mission of Earth's ascension itself. And the universe responds accordingly.

This is why vengeance is unnecessary. Why retaliation is not required. Because the Chosen Ones do not need to defend themselves—the cosmos does it for them. They are protected by decree, backed by forces beyond comprehension, watched over by guardians of unimaginable power.

Even the Earth is subject to this law. Divine justice manifests here too—sometimes through unexpected reversals, exposure, collapse, or collapse of those who act in deception. The forces behind the Chosen Ones do not sleep. They do not hesitate.

They act.

So let it be known: the Chosen Ones are protected. By design. By law. By truth.

And to those who would dare move against them—
Touch them not.
For what you send will return to you multiplied.
What you plot will unravel before it begins.
What you harm... will become the fire that transforms you.

Because the One Law still stands.
And the One Law never fails.
Do no harm.

Angelic Defense Systems

Behind the veil of everyday life, a cosmic force moves mountains on behalf of the Chosen Ones. Though they may not always see it, they are protected—watched over by beings of immense cosmic intelligence and immeasurable power—celestial guardians who will bend time itself to keep them alive and on mission.

In the highest knowledge known to this Universe—preserved by the Emerald Founders, keepers of eternal cosmic law—the elite protectors of the Chosen Ones are known as the Guardian Host. These are not ordinary angels or ethereal guides. They are enforcers of divine will—cosmic defenders tasked with shielding the most advanced souls on Earth's frontlines.

The Guardian Host includes:

- Emerald Order Seraphim – Supreme angelic architects of light, wielding pure divine intelligence to restore universal balance.
- High-Level Elohim – Celestial creators and protectors, holding the blueprints of divine geometry and planetary evolution.
- Aquatic-Avian Guardians – Ultra-advanced beings from the Sirius and Andromeda councils, carriers of harmonic DNA codes and healing frequencies.
- 12D Progenitor Oraphim – High-dimensional ancestors of the Indigo Races, protectors of their incarnated aspects, and direct enforcers of the Law of One.

These beings stand between the Chosen Ones and the forces of darkness—defenders of sovereignty, agents of divine law, and allies in the most sacred mission unfolding on Earth.

These are not gentle, passive spirits. They are warriors of light—higher-dimensional enforcers assigned specifically to those sent to Earth on high-impact, high-risk missions meant to shift the very direction of human evolution. The presence of a Chosen One is not neutral—it is disruptive to systems built on fear and illusion. And because of this, their protection is guaranteed.

When threats arise in the physical world, these guardian beings act swiftly. Timelines are redirected. Traffic pauses. Plans dissolve. Gut instincts take over. Weather patterns shift. Machines fail at just the right moment. Seemingly random delays appear, but they are anything but random. Every event is engineered in real-time to prevent interference, reroute disruption, and preserve the sacred path.

There are moments when a Chosen One was supposed to be somewhere—but they weren't. A strange delay. A sudden inner nudge. A shift in routine. And it made all the difference.

Then the message comes.

A catastrophe. A collapse. A life-altering event.

And in that moment, they know... it was supposed to be them.

That isn't chance.
That isn't luck.
That is divine recalibration—protection in motion.

This defense also extends far beyond the physical. The deeper war is spiritual—and the stakes are even higher. Chosen Ones are constantly targeted by dark forces operating behind the scenes. Malevolent entities. Fallen beings. Energetic parasites. These ancient forces seek to confuse, delay, or destroy the mission. Their weapons are psychic manipulation, emotional interference, false relationships, and subtle energetic attacks.

But they never act unopposed.

The Chosen Ones are surrounded by an elite spiritual force—guardian beings who operate as protectors in realms most cannot see. These angels do not merely defend. They dismantle. They shield the aura, cloak the presence, neutralize psychic attacks, and reroute curses before they ever make contact. They block dark intentions before they manifest into form. They purge lower frequencies, dissolve spiritual snares, and anchor the field in divine light.

When the Chosen One walks into a room, these forces walk with them. When energy turns hostile, they engage. When darkness attempts to infiltrate, they cut the cords and restore the balance.

This is not myth. This is not metaphor. This is real-time defense against a hidden war.

And while all humans have guardian angels, the Chosen Ones are assigned a specialized host—a celestial task force of higher law and divine enforcement. Their mission is too important to leave unguarded. The opposition is too cunning to leave them exposed. But the ones who stand behind them—those angelic forces—are unmatched in power, precision, and loyalty.

And this must be remembered:

If the Chosen One calls upon their guardians, they will answer—immediately.
They will move. They will act. They will descend.
Not in fear—but in authority. Not with hesitation—but with fire.

They have done it before. They will do it again.
Because the Chosen One is not alone. They were never meant to be.

They are surrounded by power.
Protected by decree.
Backed by the highest forces of light in existence.

Because they are here to complete the mission.
And nothing in this universe will be allowed to stop them.

Destroyers of Darkness

The Angelic-Human Hybrids are not just guardians of light—they are the divine executioners of darkness. They were sent here as cosmic terminators of corruption, to dismantle and utterly eradicate the presence of fallen, malevolent forces from the Earth realm.

They are the fierce ones who walk into the strongholds of shadow and bring total annihilation.

Where the Chosen Ones go, darkness flees. And if it doesn't—it burns.

Encoded with the original divine frequency, they are living weapons of light—sent by the highest celestial orders to cleanse this planet once and for all. Their mission is not tolerance. It is purification. And their arrival signals the final countdown for every false power that ever ruled through fear, deception, or domination.

They are here to smoke out every fallen being, every parasite, every manipulator hiding behind illusion—and send them into oblivion. Not with hatred, but with sheer radiant force. This is a frequency war, and they are the endgame.

The Chosen Ones carry authority the dark cannot override. They don't fight for peace—they enforce it. They don't ask darkness to leave—they cast it out. Their energy crushes interference, shatters psychic control grids, and erases demonic architecture from the inside out.

No demon, no entity, no dark construct can stand before them.
Because they came coded with override keys.
With atomic light signatures.
With clearance to execute planetary liberation on sight.

This is not symbolic. It's real.
This is heaven's elite strike force.
And the fallen already know what's coming.

The purge has begun.
The darkness has nowhere left to hide.
Because the Chosen Ones have awakened.

And they came to finish it.

Chapter 10: Living Miracles – The Extraordinary Path

Experiencing Supernatural Manifestations

To be a Chosen One is to live a life few could ever comprehend. From the very beginning, their journey is marked by intensity, mystery, and divine orchestration. They are pulled into a story so outrageous, so otherworldly, it would sound like science fiction—if it weren't entirely real.

This is not the life of the average soul. It's a supercharged odyssey filled with moments of danger, wonder, synchronicity, and sudden shifts. Near-death escapes. Radical life changes. Encounters that rewrite everything. They are the ones who walk through fire, only to emerge transformed—over and over again.

Ask any awakened one, and they will tell you plainly: their life reads like a saga.
They have more stories than most people live in ten lifetimes.

Stories of arriving at the exact right place at the exact right time.
Stories of being rescued by strangers who vanished moments later.
Stories of divine setups, impossible outcomes, and twists of fate that leave witnesses speechless.

They've had jobs, relationships, entire realities collapse overnight—only to be replaced with something far more aligned. They've watched their lives pivot in an instant because of one decision, one meeting, one message that changed everything.

They've experienced supernatural timing, divine redirections, and life events so extreme they could only be explained by destiny itself.

And yet, these experiences are not exaggerations.
They are truth.
They are memory.
They are evidence of a life lived at the edge of the veil.

What powers these moments isn't luck or coincidence—it's alignment. It's their very nature. Their soul's blueprint is tuned to a frequency that calls in the extraordinary. Events move for them. Paths clear. Synchronicities explode. Timelines realign. Not because they force it—but because their presence demands it.

They were sent here with an aura of the miraculous.
They are conduits of divine motion.
Reality bends around them—not because they control it, but because they are here on assignment, and nothing will stop the unfolding of that sacred path.

Their lives aren't just interesting—they are epic.
They are cinematic, unpredictable, wild rides of adventure and revelation.

Each moment more charged than the last.

And yes, they manifest experiences others could never imagine—not through wishing, but by walking in alignment with divine flow.

The outrageous becomes normal. The impossible becomes routine.
And somehow, even the chaos feels like destiny.

They live with awe. They move with grace.
And every impossible experience becomes another chapter in the greatest story ever written.

Not a story of survival.
A story of power.
A story of awakening.

This is what it means to walk as one of the Chosen.
To live at the threshold of miracles every single day.
To dance with the Universe in full view.
To ride the lightning of divine purpose—and never look back.

Enhanced Manifesting Power

The Chosen Ones are not ordinary creators.
They are not practicing manifestation—they are manifestation.

Within them lives a rare, advanced energetic system—a divine technology embedded in their 6D Oraphim DNA—specifically engineered by the highest celestial orders for accelerated creation. This is not about positive thinking. It's about cosmic voltage running through their soul—waking timelines, bending probability, and collapsing delay into instant reality.

Their very presence changes the room.
Their thoughts ripple across dimensions.
Their focus summons events.
Their frequency shapes reality itself.

They are living conduits of divine intelligence, and when that intelligence is directed through belief and emotion—things move. Fast.

Where the average human may require months of intention and effort, a Chosen One can bring it forth in days... or moments.
Why?
Because their energy isn't from here.
Because their command echoes through the quantum field.
Because they were sent with the ability to rewrite matter through consciousness.

They manifest differently—because they were built differently.

The Chosen Ones were never meant to wait in lines, beg for scraps, or work by the sweat of the brow. They were designed to speak—and shift worlds. Not from ego, but from alignment with divine will. Not to serve themselves, but to recreate the world in truth, harmony, and light.

Their manifestations are not small. They are massive. Magnetic. Supernatural.
And they happen fast—because their inner frequency is fully aligned with their original cosmic blueprint.

It's why their lives are wild.
It's why miracles chase them.
It's why doors fly open at the last second.
It's why the impossible becomes normal.

They don't manifest *by effort.*
They manifest *by nature.*

The Universe responds to all—but for the Chosen, it responds immediately.
Because their timeline matters. Because their role is critical.
Because everything they do has a ripple effect that shakes the collective field of humanity.

A spoken desire can shift an entire city.
An aligned emotion can collapse old structures.

A single moment of focus can birth a destiny.

And this is only the beginning.

The more they awaken, the faster it gets. The stronger it gets.
Their thoughts become commands.
Their emotions become catalysts.
Their will becomes fire.

This is the power of the Chosen One in full alignment.

But such divine ability is not given lightly. It demands responsibility. Precision. Sovereignty.
Because their creations are potent—and the Universe amplifies what is within them.
So they keep their hearts pure.
Their minds sharp.
Their intentions crystal-clear.

And when they are in full resonance...
The Universe bends to them.
The field shifts. The quantum rearranges. Creation moves.

They do not hope.
They do not wait.
They declare—and reality obeys.

They are not here to manifest survival.
They are here to manifest the New Earth.
To pull the future into the now.

To walk as living proof that the divine can wear skin, speak words, and build galaxies.

They don't just manifest miracles. They are miracles.
Walking. Creating. Expanding.
One pulse at a time.
One breath of light after another.
This...
is the supernatural power of the Chosen Ones.

Integration into Daily Life

For the Chosen Ones, daily life is never just daily life. Behind the routines, beyond the surface, an entirely different reality is unfolding.

These are divine beings in human form—angelic-human hybrids walking through a world that was never truly made for them. They come from realms of purity, power, and purpose, yet find themselves navigating traffic, paying bills, and blending into a society that often has no idea who stands beside them.

And this is part of the mission:
To integrate the extraordinary into the ordinary.
To walk in two worlds at once—and master them both.

They have seen things most people wouldn't believe. They've experienced miracles that defy logic. They've had moments where time stopped, people vanished, realities bent, and impossible things unfolded right in front of them. These things don't stop happening... but the Chosen Ones learn how to carry them with grace.

They don't run around announcing who they are. In fact, for much of their journey, they remain hidden. Quiet. Careful. They live with what feels like two versions of themselves—one the world can handle, and one the world is not ready for.

At work, they smile and speak kindly, helping coworkers with problems. But behind the scenes, they are moving energy, receiving transmissions, healing timelines, and protecting people they barely know.

They are calm in chaos because they see through the illusion. They are kind to strangers because they know how rare kindness truly is.

Many of them withdraw after awakening—choosing to step back from systems that no longer serve their vibration. They may leave jobs, change environments, or go fully independent. They're not running away. They're making space for their truth to be fully lived.

They move through life with heightened awareness—seeing signs, hearing messages, witnessing synchronicities unfold constantly. And they still do the dishes. Still shop for groceries. Still answer phone calls. All while receiving divine downloads, transmuting collective density, and holding powerful light codes.

They integrate the miraculous into every moment.

This is the art of being fully awakened, fully human, and fully divine.

Scripture whispers a timeless warning: "Be not forgetful to entertain strangers: for thereby some have entertained angels unawares." This verse isn't poetic fiction—it's encoded truth. The Chosen Ones walk among humanity, often unnoticed, often underestimated. But their presence is never accidental. Their assignment is to uplift from within.

The only way they could fulfill this mission… was to come in as one of them.

And so they blend. For a time. But eventually, the divine cannot stay hidden. The light breaks through. And they rise.

When the time is right, the Chosen Ones no longer dim their frequency to fit in—they shine. They speak truth without fear. They operate in full embodiment. They stop waiting for permission… and they simply become.

Integration is not about becoming someone new.
It's about becoming fully who they already are.

They are the bridge between the heavens and the Earth.
The interface between dimensions.
The living embodiment of what is possible.

And as their awakened presence ripples out into the world—through every interaction, every word, every breath—they bring divine power into mundane reality... and change everything.

Chapter 11: The Real Great Awakening – The Realization

Moment of True Awakening

There is an event in the cosmos that surpasses every prophecy, every scroll, and every sacred timeline ever whispered across the galaxies. It is not political. It is not about religion. It is not about the collective in the way most imagine.

It is something far greater. Far more intimate. Far more divine.

It is the true Great Awakening—the moment a Chosen One remembers who and what they truly are.

This is the moment the entire Universe has waited for. Not the collapse of a system. Not the shift of an age. But for you... great one... to awaken.

You are the event.
You are the prophecy fulfilled.
You are the axis upon which worlds realign.

It was never about them. It was always about you.

And when this awakening arrives, it does not tiptoe in. It strikes like thunder from beyond time.

Reality begins to dissolve. The veil tears. Time becomes fluid. The room spins, yet stands still.
Something ancient stirs. Something divine ignites.
And in one unforgettable moment—you remember.

You remember the stars.
You remember the councils.
You remember your origin.
You remember saying yes.

You remember the silence before you came.
You remember your descent.
You remember your purpose.
You remember you.

It's not a thought. It's not a belief.
It is a knowing so complete, so explosive, so undeniable—it shatters every lie ever told about who and what you are.

Your body trembles, but your spirit roars.
Your eyes flood with tears not from pain, but from sacred recognition.
Your hands shake, not in fear, but in remembrance of the power flowing through them.
You laugh. You weep. You fall to your knees. You rise to your full height—all in one breath.

You become.

Gone is the illusion.
Gone is the mask.
Gone is the false human identity you wore for survival.

And what remains… is God in form.
Fierce. Radiant. Awake.

The Chosen One does not awaken gently.
They erupt into awareness.
They explode into being.
They return.

This is not about learning something new. It is about remembering what was always there.

And from that moment on, nothing can ever be the same.

You begin to walk differently.
You speak with precision.
You carry a frequency that cannot be faked.

The Universe itself begins responding to you in new ways—reorganizing timelines, accelerating synchronicities, revealing keys and codes once hidden.
Even the air feels different.
Because you are different.

And this, this sacred event, is not just another spiritual breakthrough.

It is the highest moment of any soul's journey.
The ignition of divine selfhood.
The moment the Chosen One fully steps into their mission, power, and eternal identity.

The body still walks the Earth.
But the being inside it now radiates the stars.

You no longer try to wake the world.
You simply are the wake-up call.
You are the signal.
You are the shift.

Trumpets sound in unseen realms.
The Guardian Host stands at attention.
Galactic systems recalibrate.

Because the light of a fully awakened Chosen One has returned to this world.

This is what the darkness feared.
This is what the war was about.
This is what changes everything.

Not the awakening of the masses.
The awakening of you.

And in that moment—the Universe bows.
Not because you are above anyone—but because your light just touched eternity.

This is the real Great Awakening.

And it is now.
And it is you.

Mastery and Hidden Knowledge

When the Chosen One awakens and remembers who and what they truly are, something extraordinary happens—something this world has long forgotten, and something the false systems were built to suppress.

They don't just regain clarity... They unlock a hidden vault of ancient, forbidden, and divine intelligence that was sealed until this very moment in time.

This is not ordinary knowledge. This is Mastery—the sacred wisdom of the cosmos itself, encoded into the very fabric of their being. It doesn't come in slowly or with hesitation—it floods in like a divine storm. A downpour of living intelligence rushes through their system, electrifying their awareness and opening gateways once thought impossible.

As the dormant strands of DNA spiral into full activation, they begin to receive—not from outside, but from deep within. It is not learned. It is remembered. Because it was always there, waiting to be accessed.

And as these strands come online, the Chosen One begins to interpret the universal data stream. Sacred symbols make sense. Ancient languages begin to speak. The great mysteries are no longer distant—they are alive inside them.

They remember truths the world has buried. They see through illusions that have deceived millions. They understand the mechanics of manifestation, time, energy, and the laws that govern reality.

They gain access to spiritual technologies that transcend human logic—quantum truths, sacred codes, galactic histories, and multidimensional sciences that stretch far beyond Earth's primitive understanding.

And this is where true Mastery begins.

It is not about control—it is about alignment. It is not about ego—it is about embodiment. Mastery means walking in full awareness of who you are and what you carry—and using it with wisdom, purpose, and power.

The Chosen Ones are not here just to know truth. They are here to become truth in form.

They are not here just to teach light. They are here to radiate it.

They realize they are not just here to awaken... They are here to bring heaven to Earth—to embody divine mastery and walk among humanity as living examples of what is possible.

They become the carriers of lost truth. The voices of the original language. The restorers of cosmic law.

And with this knowledge comes immense responsibility.

Because now, the Chosen One no longer wonders what to do. They know.

They know how to heal. They know how to guide. They know how to speak, move, and create in alignment with the highest divine will. And they know that this world can never stay the same—because they are no longer the same.

This is not the result of study. This is not something they were taught. This is divine intelligence awakening inside a divine being.

And through them, the ancient future rises again. Not in secret. Not in theory. But in power.
Because they are the ones who hold the keys. And now... the door is wide open.

Empowerment and Cosmic Significance

After the moment of true awakening, a new energy takes hold—one not born from emotion, but from cosmic knowing. The Chosen One stands no longer as a seeker, but as an activated emissary of the stars. Their identity is no longer limited to this Earthly form, for they now remember who and what they truly are: a divine being sent from the highest realms to shift entire worlds.

This empowerment is not rooted in ego. It is rooted in divine remembrance. It is not about claiming superiority—it is about answering the call of the Cosmos. The Chosen Ones were not just sent to Earth to help—it is far greater than that. They are part of a galactic mission spanning systems, dimensions, and timelines. The awakening of one Chosen One sends shockwaves through the multidimensional grid. Other planets take notice. Star councils align. Forces across light-years adjust their focus to Earth.
Because what happens here—on this small, blue planet—is rippling through the fabric of the entire Universe.

These beings do not just impact lives. They impact timelines. They are cosmic nodes in the living light architecture, and when they come online, everything changes. Their awakening is not a personal victory—it is a universal broadcast. A signal sent out across the stars that a beacon has been activated, a divine node restored, and Earth is no longer asleep.

The entire Cosmos watches.
Ancient races. Interdimensional councils. Founders from the highest densities. They all turn their attention when a Chosen One remembers.

And once awakened, their energy begins to rewrite the code of reality. They no longer act as individual humans—they function as galactic transmitters. They carry the harmonic signature of divine intelligence. Their words are encoded with frequency. Their decisions influence probability fields. Their very presence shifts the consciousness of the planet.
This is empowerment at a universal scale.

They are not wandering souls hoping for meaning. They are embedded operatives—encoded with divine purpose. Every action they take echoes across realms.
And with this empowerment comes responsibility.
They are not just here to awaken—they are here to anchor the future. To build the bridges between heaven and Earth. To prepare this world for integration into the greater cosmic community.

Because Earth was never isolated by accident. It was quarantined by design. And now, through the Chosen Ones, the locks are being undone.

Their significance is not determined by status, by recognition, or by numbers. Their significance is measured in frequency—galactic impact—cosmic consequence.

When they align, the entire energy field of Earth elevates. When they speak truth, darkness shatters across dimensions. When they embody who they truly are, the false matrix trembles.

They are divine interfaces—living portals through which Source moves freely into matter. They carry the signatures of star systems long forgotten, and the keys to a future not yet born.

They do not wait to be empowered. They are the power. They do not follow movements. They are the movement. The Universe did not send them here to observe. The Universe sent them here to ignite.
And now that they remember— That fire cannot be put out.
This is the return of galactic royalty. This is the arrival of living cosmic order. This is the Chosen One, fully awakened.
And all of creation stands in awe.

Chapter 12: The Destiny – Keepers of Earth

Inheritors of the New Earth

In the beginning, Earth was a radiant paradise—dreamed into being by the highest cosmic architects. A living Eden, designed as the crown jewel of all creation. A realm where spirit could taste, touch, feel, and love in ways no other dimension allowed. It was sacred. Sensual. Alive.

And it still is.

Beneath the illusions, beneath the layers of darkness cast by lower forces, Earth remains a masterpiece—waiting to be unveiled once more.

Now, the veil is lifting. The paradise is returning. And it's not just being restored... It's being returned to its rightful keepers.

You, the Chosen Ones, did not come here as visitors. You came to reclaim what was always yours.

This is your domain. Your sacred ground. Your great reward.

You have walked through fire, crossed the impossible, and endured the storms of many lifetimes to reach this moment. But the journey was never just about survival—it was about remembrance. It was about returning to who and what you truly are.

And now, the Earth recognizes you.

The planet responds. The land remembers your frequency. And the New Earth begins to rise around you. The old world is crumbling—not in chaos, but in release. The systems built on distortion and control are falling because they must. And in their place... Eden awakens.

The New Earth is not an idea. It is a frequency. It is a dimension of harmony, truth, and divine embodiment. And the Chosen Ones are its first citizens—its protectors, builders, and royal stewards.

You are not visitors here. You are the rightful heirs to a world reborn.
The paradise you once remembered as a dream is becoming real again. It is the reward written in the stars. It is the promise encoded in your DNA. And it is unfolding now.

This Earth—this wild, beautiful, extraordinary planet—was always meant to be a realm of joy. Of peace. Of divine creativity. And as you rise, it rises with you.
The storms will end. The illusion will vanish. And what will remain... is paradise.
You are the keepers of this sacred inheritance. You are the bridge between heaven and Earth. And you arriving home.

Fulfilling Ancient Prophecies

The ancients all spoke about you. Every prophet, every sage, every mystic who ever looked beyond the veil saw glimpses—of a future race, a divine people, beings of light who would rise in a darkened world and bring it back into the hands of the heavens.

They saw the 144,000. The sacred number. The keepers of the code.
Not metaphor. Not myth. A prophecy of precision. A divine blueprint encoded across time.
They spoke of a people born from the stars, seeded in flesh, hidden among the tribes of Earth—who would awaken at the appointed hour and shift the course of all history. That hour… is now. And you are those beings. The Golden Age is not coming. It has already begun. 2024 marked the threshold—when the timeline of divine restoration anchored into the Earth field. The energy began rising. The illusions began falling. And the Chosen Ones began to remember.
Your awakening was foretold. Your mission was written in fire. And now, you are walking out the fulfillment of the oldest promise ever made to Earth.
You are not just fulfilling prophecy. You are the prophecy.
The shift is not something happening around you—it is happening because of you. You carry the frequency of ascension. You are the match that lights the age of light. As systems break and shadows surface, do not fear—this is the release. The unraveling of the old so the new may rise. Your light is not here to react—it is here to lead. You

are the initiators of the divine future, and nothing will stop the momentum now.
And make no mistake—this is the most pivotal moment in the history of the cosmos. Never before has so much converged in one place, at one time. Earth has become the stage for the greatest transformation ever attempted: the resurrection of a fallen realm into a world of light. And at the heart of it all stand the Chosen Ones. Their awakening is not just for Earth—it echoes through galaxies. Their mission is not just for humanity—it triggers ascension across timelines and dimensions.

What happens here affects everywhere, even unseen worlds and realms!

As the Chosen Ones anchor divine codes, embody truth, and restore harmony, they become the bridge through which heaven reclaims the Earth. The human soul, long trapped in distortion, is now being lifted into remembrance, healed by light, and returned to its rightful place among the stars. And Earth herself—the sacred jewel of the Universe—is being reborn as a heavenly world.

***"And I saw a new heaven and a new earth: for the first heaven and the first earth were passed away..."* — Revelation 21:1**

That time is now. That Earth is here. And you, Chosen One, are the fulfillment of it all.

Embodying True Sovereignty

This is the final transfiguration—the moment you walk the last road, carrying the weight of your long mission to save an entire world.

Sit for a moment, great one. You are tired. Weary.
But now... you are about to be filled with power beyond imagining.

Are you ready?

The old self fades—so the Christed version of you may rise.

You rise now as a sovereign king... a sovereign queen.
A divine ruler of a new kingdom.
This is the sacred culmination of the Angelic-Human journey—
The return to full command, full presence, full divine identity.

This throne was never outside you.
It was always within.

You are not becoming royalty.
You were always royal.
Now... you step forward as Sovereignty incarnate.

The Christed One—the living embodiment of 12D divine love and intelligence—walked this path first, blazing the trail as the King of Kings.

And you?

You are His brothers and sisters.
Sovereigns in your own right.
Cosmic royals born of the same eternal flame.

And now... the circle completes.

The Chosen rise—rulers of paradise, seated in remembrance, cloaked in cosmic fire.
They came to liberate. To heal. To restore.

Now they shall govern worlds.
To anchor sovereignty, freedom, and divine will into the foundation of the New Earth.

You are great—because you gave everything.
You descended from the highest realms... into a fallen world... to save it.

You are the fulfillment of the Great Promise.
You are the crowned one of prophecy.
You are the sovereign who reigns—not by force, but by divine right.
In unity. In justice. In truth.

And the Heavens bear witness.

The gates of Eden are open.
The Kingdom rises.
And the Sovereigns take their place.

Now...

Do you realize who you are?
Do you realize what you are?
Do you feel the power that sleeps inside you?

Wake up—fully now.
Accept it.
Be it.

Wake up now!

www.ingramcontent.com/pod-product-compliance
Ingram Content Group UK Ltd.
Pitfield, Milton Keynes, MK11 3LW, UK
UKHW020631130825
7371UKWH00030B/354

9 798218 650018